The Business Startup Guide To Become An Entrepreneur

Bharat Bhuval Nishad

Published by Bharat Bhuval Nishad, 2024.

Table of Contents

Copyright

The Business Startup Guide To Become An Entrepreneur

Learn To Find Great Business Startup Ideas And Grow Your Startup By Standing Out With Innovation & Business Branding

About

Creating a startup is a hard endeavor. For everyone involved. However, there are some injustices that may occur.

Within the startup itself (among founders and employees), with clients, investors, and in the broader ecosystem. It's important to know which types of manipulation occur, as well as how each type can be leveraged in a startup environment. This is what this Book will cover.

Let Me Tell You... Everything: Some people - including me - love to know what they're getting in a package. And by this, I mean, EVERYTHING that is in the package. If you think this Book is a fit and can take your knowledge of how to protect yourself from manipulation to the next level... it would be a pleasure to have you as a student. See on the other side!

Introduction

This Book is a very simple goal. We are going to cover all of the different types of manipulation that other people can use against you so that you can better protect yourself. And we are going to cover several dimensions: emotional manipulation, fact manipulation, ID manipulation and many others. Without further ado, let's just take a moment to see what are the goals of this Book as well as the structure. Hi, and welcome to this Book on how manipulation works for all this Book. Our biggest goal is going to be to illustrate the different ways in which manipulation is used.

It includes, among other methods, how cognitive biases are explored by manipulators, false contrasts, mental effort, ability, biases, likeability in others, how manipulating someone through pressure is used, emotional blackmail, intimidation, creating false , among others. How facts themselves are the start of having different standards, contrasting things to change their apparent value and more how identification can manipulate, making someone feel understood artificially or using fake commonalities among many other methods. By the end of this Book, you will be more adept at identifying and stopping manipulation whenever it's used around you or on you in order to explore how manipulation works. We are going to cover nine key ways in which nine key types are used.

The first is consistency, manipulation. In short, when we say or do something, we are more likely to act in accordance with it. This is consistency. We don't want to contradict ourselves. So here's the key. By getting someone to state something or to do something, you change their subsequent behavior to a degree because they can't contradict themselves. Then comes Google, emotional manipulation, having emotional reactions in making the other side identify with them and take the blame for them. Bullying, emotional, blackmail, crying, asking for mercy and others, making the other side feel guilty for your emotions after that effort manipulation. Most of the effort involved in something is actually mental effort.

In other words, when you think that something is effortful, it is. And when you think that it isn't, well, it isn't. So here's the key. If you change how much effort something seems to be, you change whether people do it or not. Then standard manipulation or in other words, doing unfair comparisons, having a certain set of standards for one person or thing and different criteria for another one. These changes of the value at each one of them seem to have, because in reality, they weren't really compared in a fair manner. After that, pressure, manipulation, in short, pressuring people, intimidating them, creating false scarcity to drive urgency in other ways, to pressure them into making a decision when they're not really prepared.

After that comes identification, manipulation, in short, making the other side feel understood or similar to you in some way to artificially create a commonality and make them trust you more, which makes them drop their guard after that becomes fact manipulation. Very simple. Altering, obfuscating or simply lying about facts changes them, which makes people look at them in a different way. You can embellish facts or you can just outright lie. After that comes the true manipulation superweapon, which is context manipulation. By changing what you compare something to, you change its value.

If you change the options or if you highlight different things about the options, you can make any specific one of them look excellent or terrible. Just due to the comparison in finally labeling manipulation by attributing specific names or labels to a person or thing. You can reduce them to that label, which usually sticks in the long term, and it even resists evidence against it. You can use this to reduce a person or a thing to a specific label. It's one of the most devastating types. So now that you know what our goals are, as well as the types of manipulation that we are going to explore. Well, without further ado. Let's dive right into them.

Consistency Manipulation

Let's talk about the principle of consistency, manipulation. This principle is very simple. If the fans say that when you get someone to say that they're going to do something or take an action, they are more likely to act in accordance to it in the future, because we never want to contradict ourselves. So someone can just get you to say, I like this or I'm going to do this or I want this, and you're going to be a lock in that consistency unless you realize that. In fact, let's take a look. Consistency. Manipulation is very simple. It consists of forcing a person to commit to something or at least take action towards something, which makes them more likely to keep investing in it. This is due to the psychological principle of consistency.

It dictates that we don't like to contradict ourselves. We want to keep consistent. So once we commit to something initially, either with words or with inaction, we will tend to keep going in that direction. This creates what's known as a consistency track. This is why, for example, a charity will get you to sign a petition. And if you sign it, you're going to be much more likely to donate or to take further action. There is a line with that. There are several ways to leverage this principle for manipulation. One is active choice. When you ask a question, instead of the answers being reactive, such as a yes or no, they should be active in the first person. Such as? I will do this or I will not do this. The weight of the person saying it in the first person is much bigger. Also, escalation of commitment.

Asking for the person to take a small action, to then ask for a bigger one and just keep ramping the person up the ladder. The example that we just mentioned of the charity. Another example is just getting people to take action toward something. If they take initiative towards something, they like it more. For example, contests. Getting someone to write a slogan should a venue or other is to get a product makes them like it more. Or the IKEA effect. When you assemble a product yourself, you might get more just because of the initiative that you took in assembling it. Another example, habits. If you get someone to do something once or twice.

Chances are they are likely to continue doing it, especially for bad habits. This type of manipulation works by usually requesting the person to initially say or do something that the manipulator wants, and then they simply leverage that existing commitment to keep them going in the same direction. It's almost inertia if they take the first step. They just keep on going in the same direction. For example, a salesman asks the person to state what they like about a product or to tell them why they like it or even get them to use it. All of these actions create consistency. They make the person like the product more. Another cognitive bias that supports this is a rationalization. In short, we all have a tendency to originally do things emotionally and then later try to justify them with logic.

For example, you buy a car on a whim and then afterwards you say, oh, I'm sure that at the time I had a good reason to buy it. Definitely. Or you even fabricate facts in a lie to yourself saying something like, oh, I think that at the time it was one of the best cars in that class. In other words, we do things because we want to. Or for random reasons. Later, we pretended that we had a reason all along. So when you do or state something. Always ask yourself. By taking this action, is the other side going to force me to act in alignment with this? What are some examples of consistency? Manipulation. The first is terms of service. You will notice that many contracts in terms of service have a part where you must state in the first person.

I commit to this or I will do this. They are leveraging this principle. What you stated in the first person, you are much more likely to obey these terms. I mean, assuming you pay attention when you actually sign it. But you know where I'm going with this, right. And the other example is NGOs, as we just discussed, specifically for escalation of commitment. First, they get you to take a small action. Just visit the website or just sign a petition. And now that you've joined the cause to ask for more and more signs, they joined this group, donate a bit, do it a lot and so on. And look, when I mentioned manipulation, in many cases, charities are manipulating you for a good reason. Right? They help the planet or help animals or others. I'm just mentioning the theoretical principle, OK, in finally clarifying words, when someone gives you the answer in, you don't know what the intention is.

You might ask point blank, just be clear with me. What would you do or would you not do? Forcing the person to state it in the first person, for example, you're asking for a raise. And the person is being kind of vague. And you say, look, just be honest with me. Are you going to give me the raise or are you not going to give me the raise? Any force, the person to state that I will give you the raise or I will not give you the raise. What are our key takeaways here? The first is that consistency works because you don't want to contradict yourself. Nobody does. So in other words, if you just get someone to state or do something, they'll keep going in that direction.

It can be triggered with both words and actions. Consistency works by both getting someone to take an action or say that they will do something, both types of commitment work and both have very similar effects. And finally, rationalization helps. Here we are. All do things emotionally and then try to find a reason for them afterwards. Consistency takes advantage of this. So one gets you to do something, even if for a random reason. But when you look back at it, you try to find a logical justification for it. And consistency takes advantage of this. So as we see, consistency, manipulation is very dangerous, because if someone just gets you to take one small action or save that you are associated with something or that you like it. You may not even realize that you're being placed in a consistency trap. And even if you do realize it, you have to actively go against it, which is counterintuitive.

Consistency Manipulation in Startups

Consistency, manipulation is something that can be easily leveraged in startups, either for words or actions. The rationale is that by getting their employees to agree on the founder's ideals or a vision for not just employees, but anybody external such as clients or investors, the founder makes them more likely to act in agreement with them or, in other words, more likely to support them later. Also, by getting an investor to actively state that they agree with their vision, their business model or the overall startup, or to take actual action towards it.

For example, visiting the offices and meeting the team may make them more likely to invest. It sunk the cost of BIAs. This can also be used in any other context. So a startup can make a partner state that they want to do business with them or justify why giving reasons or they can get clients to take action towards being clients such as participating in contests, doing reviews or taking other actions. All of these are consistency traps.

Emotional Manipulation

Let's talk about good old emotional manipulation. You may think that emotional manipulation is just emotional blackmail. For example, having a negative reaction, crying or throwing a tantrum and getting to the other side to change reactions because of that. And that is true. But there are other types of emotional manipulation. For example, twisting the knife, creating panic in someone, pushing their buttons just to get them to take action or doing the precise opposite. For example, building hype and want in something. Desire. All of these different techniques can create emotions in a person and get them to take an action that they would otherwise not take if they didn't have those emotions.

Let's take a look. Emotional manipulation is any type of behavior that makes people take different actions due to feeling responsible for the emotions of others. When I mention this, you may immediately think of emotional blackmail, and that is a perfect example, but it's not the only case at all. This type of manipulation can come in the following firm's first building, hiding in getting someone to feel positive feelings about something that may not be justified at all. That's also a type of emotional manipulation. Then you have the flip side of this effect, twisting the knife, making someone feel really bad about something in order to get them to take action. For example, a salesperson illustrating the nightmare scenario to get the person to buy.

If you don't buy this weight loss pill, are you willing to be overweight 20 years from now with nobody loving you? That kind of thing? Then the usual case, bullying or emotional blackmail? The person being aggressive or intimidating in getting their person to change their action by throwing a tantrum, gifting them, being needy or others, and finally just triggering fear and panic in the person used a lot by politicians, but also by shock news. Getting you to take some kind of action because you're just afraid. This type of manipulation works for one very specific reason, which is associated reactions. By this, I mean the following.

Under normal circumstances, we don't identify with someone's reactions. If they become angry, if they become afraid. That's not my issue. But by talking about their situation or what happens to them, what they want or your emotions, the other side forces you to understand them. They attach themselves to you. You are not responsible for their reactions. This is a Woodway hoboing work. The other side is aggressive. And on top of it, they make you feel guilty for what you're doing. Naturally, people with a high degree of empathy or just have low self-esteem, get manipulated more easily.

But if the manipulator really drives up the guilty, anyone can fall prey to this. What are some examples of emotional manipulation? The first is bullying. As we mentioned, this is the simplest example of emotional manipulation. The other side reacts violently to get you to take the blame for their reaction. You feel responsible for someone else's reaction, which actually has nothing to do with you. Pity and Kamasi are another example when someone does something wrong and asks you for mercy. For example, if they made a serious mistake at work and they want you to not fire them, they're essentially trying to make you feel responsible for them in finally attention seeking behavior.

People that display this kind of behavior are doing exactly this. They act emotional and they do extreme things just to get the attention of others. What are our key takeaways here? The first is that it's all about the reaction. Emotional manipulation is all about having a specific reaction in making the other person feel guilty for it. You attach yourself to them in a way. This can happen to anyone. Naturally, people understand. Others to a higher degree can fall prey to this more frequently.

But anyone, regardless of their conditions, can feel guilty for the reactions of others. If the manipulation is just intense enough, there are different types here. But any type of emotional attitude by the other person can be manipulated if they are trying to blame you for it. Bullying, pity, attention seeking, pouting, crying winds or any other type of reaction can fit here. So as we see, all the different types of emotional manipulation are very dangerous. If you don't realize that someone is holding you responsible for your emotions or actively changing, then you are going to take a different action because of those emotions.

Emotional Manipulation in Startups

Emotional manipulation can be very present in the startup world, and especially then by the founders if they are more emotional by nature. There are some founders that are objective, but a lot of founders are too visionary and detached from reality. This is because the startup world itself, in the nature of the job, attracts people with strong vision and in many cases that are disconnected from reality, which can make them persistent, but can also make them stubborn, in denial and possibly rejecting proof that goes against them. So this means that the founder can be very emotionally manipulative in terms of forcing employees to attempt things that everybody knows are not going to work out just out of wishful thinking, or they can frequently change their mind and forget that they even said something or say one thing when they meant another, or they can take ownership for the ideas of others or they can pressuring employees into very strict deadlines. Usually they get themselves into trouble and they promise things to clients. And then the team is the one that needs to actually get out of that trouble.

Standard Manipulation in Startups

Let's talk about effort, manipulation or more specific, perceived effort manipulation. We all have a perception of how much effort something is. Right. This is a lot of effort. This is no effort. And we tend to take action based on that. So that's the key. If someone can manipulate how much effort something seems to be, they change their actions. A very known type of this is what are called convenience words or low effort words. If you just say that something is simple or quick or easy, even if it isn't, it's going to seem to be simple and quick and easy and people are more likely to do it. Let's take a look at this example and others. Most of the effort involved in doing something is actual perceived effort and not real effort.

More specifically, two thirds of the total effort is perceived, as mentioned in the book, The Effortless Experience. In short, what happens is that when you think that something is a lot of effort, then it is in when you think it isn't. Well, it isn't. For example, two different people think about crying. Bursten A says, I have to search for the clothes, get dressed, then we warm up, then stretch etc. While Person B says, just go. We have a completely different perception of effort for the exact same thing. So the chapter here is that you can manipulate the perceived effort of something which changes what people actually do. There is a set of key techniques here to achieve justice.

One method is through low effort words, using words such as easy or fast. We're seeing things like instant access or sign up now or make something seem less effortful. Another example is reducing options instead of 20 alternatives. Well, we have three or four. It's a principle called the paradox of choice. Those options that someone has, the more likely they are to take action after that, preempting doubt. For example, what effects do answering common questions if you don't know how to contact us? Call this number. If you don't know how to pay, do this. And so on. This takes situations of uncertainty and eliminates them making action less effortful.

And another method is implementation intention, using questions or statements that make the person illustrate something. How would you do this? What would it take? Was the picture in their mind? It's less effortful because they already know how to do it. Another example is to bring structure or progress into something saying it's just two steps or right. Step three for this type of manipulation works, because when something seems to be less effortful, we are more likely to do it. As we just mentioned. So anything that reduces effort actually manipulates us to be more likely to do just that.

Or if you think about it, anything that increases the perceived effort of the competition makes a person more likely to go with him. This type of manipulation in particular works very well on things that we are being introduced to. For the first time, not that much on things that we already know. For example, software products, every single software product nowadays claims to be fast and easy or just two steps. But after we've used them for a while, that effect kind of dissipates because we now know what reality is. So this works very well on things we don't know. But not that much on things that we already know. It's still there, but it's smaller. So we're being exposed to something for the first time.

It's very easy to fall into this trap. What are some examples of effort manipulation? The first is software products. Every single software product nowadays averages low effort words. As we just mentioned, using chat instead of speaking, saying that it's fast or easy or just two steps or instant access and so on, all of them make it seem easier than effet use. These are great to reduce uncertainty in the person. Every adult is an obstacle, and every answer to a doubt is a way to decrease the mental effort. The more options that you remove for the person, the less perceived effort it is. Another example, the specific one is Steve Jobs. He was great at introducing structure to his chapters.

I'm here to talk about three things. I have two things to talk about. Even if the chapter was one hour or more, it seemed very simple due to the fact that he brought structure to it. What are our key takeaways here? First, perceived effort is everything. Mental effort is two thirds of the total effort of something. So this means that when we think that something is a little effort, it is when we think that it's high effort, it is then there are multiple ways to reduce the mental effort. Anything that reduces perceived effort manipulates the person to take action more easily. Effort towards reducing options, reducing uncertainty. And finally, it's better the first time when you've known something for a while, you already know how much effort it actually is.

So these techniques don't affect you that much, but if it's the first time, you can be very easily manipulated. So as we see, effort manipulation is a very, very subtle type of manipulation. You have to actively think that the thing that seems to be low effort may actually be very high effort. And you need to be aware that someone may be guiding you to the path. It seems less effortful, even if in reality it's not less effortful at all.

Effort Manipulation in Startups

Effort manipulation is probably the most used type of manipulation in startups, specifically for marketing startup products. Put simply, startups make everything seem easier or simpler in order to grow and sell their product. Easier banks, simpler food delivery, quicker ride, hailing in so many other variations. Even if in reality, things are not easier or simpler at all. Some techniques, Minkus, first in the product coffee itself, on the landing page of every product or in its description, you will see expressions such as just two easy steps. It's quick and easy. Instant access or others.

Then in relationships or pitches, the startup is always pitched, being easy and convenient for clients or partners and for investors. So saying something like it's a very simple idea that'll grow easily or making the process itself seem easier. It's easy to invest. It's easy to buy and set up our product. It's easy to become our partner. And so what? In finally preempting doubts, problems are pre-emptive using Yaphet cues or specific web pages or other formats. There are some rectors of objections that have immediate answers. If you don't know how to pay rebates, if you don't know how to log in freebies and on.

Standard Manipulation

Let's talk about standard manipulation in this case, having two different standards for two different people or projects or elements. What you do is you judge one person or one element according to a specific set of criteria, and the other one, according to no criteria or different criteria, is a very known type of this is motivated reasoning, which essentially dictates that if we like something, we are going to judge it less. But if we don't like something, we are really going to judge it. Let's take a look at this type and more of standard manipulation. Standard manipulation simply consists of changing the requirements for something in order to make something seem better or worse. So, by the way, to clarify the worthy I don't mean standard manipulation as a normal manipulation. I mean, standard manipulation is in manipulating the standards of sampling the necessary criteria.

The example that may immediately come to mind is someone literally having the standard of having low demands of someone in high demand of another person this way. One of the two people seems higher value because in reality, the criteria that were used were different to begin with. This is very frequently used when people are favoring friends, especially in the corporate world. You measure everybody by the normal criteria in your friend by special criteria. There are several variations of this type of manipulation. The basic version is what are we changing the standards? As I mentioned, having certain standards for a person and different ones for another person.

Then we have exceptions, which is possibly the most frequent type. In some cases, you will not scrutinize someone. Everybody else follows the process. But this specific person doesn't weigh that process. They're treated in a special way. They just skip the queue. After that comes motivated reasoning. You scrutinize more. The people who you dislike motivated reasoning makes you subconsciously come up with more and more obstacles and tests for people that you don't like. It makes you trust blindly the people that you do like. Another technique is an expected rigidity when something is almost closed. You make an additional ask or have unexpected demands. For example, two people showed the same exact application.

But for one of them, you see oh, by the way, besides what's written down on the application, I need this additional information on paper. They're treated in the exact same way. But in practice, not at all. Standard manipulation is particularly dangerous when the manipulator refuses to provide transparency. In fact, it's the only condition under which this type of manipulation can even survive. For example, this is what happens in 99 percent of all skewed performance reviews. Someone is treated the wrong way compared to another person. And the key here is if you are the ones suffering from this. If you could just compare your unfair review to someone else and see the same standards, you would know that the standards were different to begin with.

But that transparency is not provided. They just tell you you have this score. This other person has a different score. In fact, the manipulator in this case makes it a point to keep every person or everything isolated and not in contact, because that's the only way that they can justify every single person not being able to compare themselves to others. Standard manipulation itself. In fact, when we work, when the manipulator is not transparent about the criteria and the only way to fight it is precisely the man's transparency on them. So it completely relies on a comparison not being available, because that allows you to hide the different standards that are used to compare different people. That's an example of an exception. If someone is an exception, you can compare them with others because there are no set rules for that person.

They're an exception. What are some examples here? The first is hiring exceptions. It makes it very clear when hiring most people apply where they see the height for a position in our company. But some are exceptions. They saw above others and have exceptions made for them. But the candidates there are competing on the side. They are in the rat race, so to speak. Never know what are the exceptions who are playing a different game altogether. The second example is motivated reasoning. Two people may be exactly the same, but if we make one of them and we dislike the other one, our criteria will be completely different.

We will scrutinize the person that we there's like so much testing them, throwing obstacles, simply not believing them. And we will completely drop our guard with a person that we like dressing them instantly in, finally. And queer performance is another example. As we just stated, a malicious manager can measure one employee with a set of criteria and then another one with different criteria, making one person seem to have a much better performance than the other. With no transparency for the people involved, what are our key takeaways here? The first is that standard manipulation, as the name implies, simply relies on changing the standards for different people or things. One person or thing gets judged in a certain way and another in a different manner.

And they're not comparable. This type of manipulation thrives in the dark. There's something very poetic, by the way. Standard manipulation can only happen by keeping the actual standards hidden, not published. The moment someone gains transparency about the standards, everything falls apart. That's why the manipulator never really mentioned the criteria that they're using because they don't want them to be compared. And finally, exceptions are notable. They are the most frequent type of standard manipulation. It's not uncommon for someone to have similar criteria for different people and just change the criteria for a specific person. It's not common at all for someone to actively use different criteria for different people.

You need to keep track of a lot of different variables. It's much more common. They have the same criteria for 90 percent of the people and then everybody else is an exception. And there are no rules for those people because they just bypass the system. So as we see, standard manipulation relies on hiding the criteria used to compare something or just not using criteria, for example, for exceptions. And that's precisely how you counter it, by forcing the person to be transparent about all of the criteria used for different people or different elements.

Standard Manipulation in Startups

Standard manipulation is extremely present in the startup world and usually not within any individual startup, but in terms of the general ecosystem. It's very unfair. So first, successful founders are hailed as geniuses, while the failing ones are usually just forgotten. If you're in the startup world, these should be common to you. It's a type of bias called survivorship bias. And this occurs despite the fact that they may have followed the same process. So maybe they took the exact same actions, but they are judged by different criteria than investment. In events, words are many times given to startups due to political reasons or to achieve certain quotas. Regardless of the actual startup quality, for example, I've seen startup events where a university is a major sponsor and they're trying to promote research projects related to clean energy.

So the winning startup is surprise, surprise, a clean energy startup. Even though it's technically good for the planet, it's still completely unfair. It's a competition. Or maybe there's an event that is sponsored by a big insurance company. And then mysteriously, most of the winners of the awards are insurance startups. So the standards in startup events may be completely corrupted, and they frequently are then even within a startup. Employees may be judged in different ways, especially if the founder is the emotional type. For example, you may be a loyal employee for five years with great results, but then you decide to challenge the founder once or disagree with them in public, for example.

And suddenly your whole past is forgotten and maybe you get fired. Naturally, this shouldn't occur with a healthy, objective startup. But hey, we're talking about manipulation, right? Or maybe even the founders themselves in certain startups like Twitter. One of the founders decides to go against the rest of the team. And they are not only kicked out with the rest of the team, they try to completely rewrite history to the weaker.

Pressure Manipulation

Let's talk about pressure, manipulation. Very simple, but very powerful. You can create artificial deadlines or you can just be intimidating or you can fake scarcity to move a person to take an action that they otherwise would not take. Why? Because they are just pressured. Let's take a look. Manipulating the pressure placed on someone is honestly such a basic form of manipulation, but it's still one of the most effective ones. In one of the most widely used ones, in short, you wave at your presence to manipulate others, to intimidate you, create tension, you create urgency, you throw the person off balance so that they won't be able to tolerate that tension. So they break easily. They rush into action that they shouldn't. There are multiple ways to achieve this, although they're very similar in nature.

The first is intimidation. Just using your personal presence this time for the other side going, for example. The second is urgency, creating deadlines or limiting the availability of a thing. Then bluffing. Bluffing is all about taking a big action that scares the other side into not reacting. Another example is a concept in politics called escalation dominance, where a concrete just keeps taking more and more extreme actions to try and dominate just due to the momentum. They don't give the other side a chance to react. This can be done by people as well. This in specific, is a type of manipulation that works very well because a lot of people in life cannot hold attention or retaliate when someone is being very intimidating. So most people just cave. But that is also precisely its fatal flaw.

The moment that someone can stand up to the manipulator and have as much presence and pressure as them or even more, then the whole thing falls apart. For example, things work very well. This is until someone calls your wife. And the same for all other times. The headlines seem very intimidating until a person looks you in the eye and rejects the bad life. And now your power is zero. This type of manipulation can be easily prevented by just not being intimidated by others. For example, asking to take your time or even being more present than the other side, holding eye contact where we're silent. What are the elements? You see this, for example, in movies or TV shows when the boy traced the boys, someone new, but then they realize that this person is very intense.

So the other person ends up intimidating the boy itself, and they were not expecting that. So it's actually just having more presence than the other side. What are some examples of pressure manipulation? The first is high pressure sales, literally days when a salesperson tries to close you on the spot right then and there they are leveraging this, using your eternality, urgency and pressure. Possibly also using other types of manipulation, such as emotional manipulation to twist the knife in you in the academic world. This happens a lot. People with a lot of tenure and reputation assume that they are important just due to their status. So in many cases, they ask for favors. They tell others what to do, and they expect zero talking back to them and people will be renting.

One person doesn't recognize their authority, and then the frame is completely broken. And finally, bosses, I'm sure that everyone knows this example, the—manager that intimidates people into doing overtime or not asking for a raise. When in reality, the person could hide it, but they just don't because they're intimidated. But again, the moment someone stands up to them before. What are our key takeaways here? The first is that there are different formats. This type of manipulation works by pressuring the person into acting right away and usually at a disadvantage. It can be for intimidation, bluffing, escalation, dominance, creating urgency or others. Or these formats work. It works because people can't take it.

If someone can't hold eye contact or is very shy, you can easily intimidate them. But it's also an issue. If the person is more intense than the manipulator, they won't be able to pressure them. And this is a great segue way to the third takeaway. The way to destroy this type of manipulation is to simply stand up to the manipulator, be more present, and that this type of manipulation only works if the person doesn't stand up to the manipulator. So if you hold the tension, take your time and even be more present than them, then you're immune.

So as we see, fighting pressure, manipulation has to do with not being pressured at the end of the day, not believing lines in scarcity or just not reacting to them and not being intimidated by people who are very present. It's selling the capacity to say, OK, you have a deadline, I'm out. I'm sorry. Or you only have a few units left. Good for you. I'm out. Or being able to lock a person in the eyes and say, you seem very intense, but unfortunately, I'm not going to let you intimidate me. Are we going to continue this as equals? This is how you fight pressure.

Pressure Manipulation in Startups

Pressure manipulation is, in fact, one of the most frequent types in the startup world, and it's used mostly by every stakeholder in almost every situation. So everybody is pressuring someone into something. Let me elaborate. In the early stages, the startup has no money, so they are both pressuring investors to invest if they can find them and pressuring clients to pay. But probably most of all, they are pressuring employees to get things done, especially if the founder has to make some bold promises with a streak that lines for their clients. And the team is the one that needs to deal with it to get things done on time. So there is a lot of artificial scarcity and cutting off exits here.

Startups pretending to be oversubscribed in the funding round to raise investor interest, telling investors they have to move immediately, creating false waiting lists to create scarcity for their clients. You name it. There are many variations here in stages, however. The investors are the ones who will be pressuring the farming team to grow in specific ways or to make certain strategic changes, such as removing the following team. Look, especially if the startup takes VC, which wants them to grow massively. But the founders don't want to grow that fast. In that case, they are not going to be aligned. And the pressure from the VC firm to force them to grow will be immense. And in many cases, it literally rips apart the startup. And naturally everything here can be done with intimidation. Jilting scarcity, even emotional blackmail, among others. As long as you pressure the other side into making a premature decision.

Identification Manipulation

Identification manipulation is very simple. It consists of faking commonalities or using empathy to seem closer to the person than you really are. I'm sure that you've heard a salesman or real estate agent say something like, Oh, so you like this football team? I like it as well. Have you gone to this game, et cetera, or. Oh, so you're having your first child. Let me tell you about the time that I have mine. What these people are doing is emphasizing the common characteristics or just creating them out of thin air. Using lies to make it seem like they're more identified with you. And because of that, you trust them more. Let's take a look at how this works.

ID manipulation, as the name says, consists of fabricating commonalities or understanding with someone in order to create a bond that isn't really there. So this makes the person subconsciously like you more. Because we all like people who are similar to us. So if the person seems to understand this or is similar to us, they'll persuade us more easily. Even if it's all fake, you might immediately think of the example of a salesman or real estate agent. They try to show you how they understand you and talk about similar life experiences just in order to sell. And it's a perfect example.

There are several techniques that average this principle. The first is empathy when it's not sincere and it's being used as a weapon. When a customer support person or an Asia representative in a company shows that they understand you just to make you feel understood. And the Zarmina, when they say, I value your time,

I'm very sorry for this and so on. Then a technical ethical labeling is similar labeling an emotion in a person decreases its intensity because it goes from emotional to logical. So when someone gets you to talk about your emotions so that you decrease the intensity of them. They are disarming that emotion. And if you're angry and you're in the corner, you'll keep being angry.

But if someone comes and says, you seem angry, you talk about it and you've let it go. And the key here is that some people get you to talk about it just so that you lose that emotion. After that, mirroring someone, mirroring your words or body language or others just to make you subconsciously like them more because they seem similar to you. It's an artificial similarity. Other types of Anup techniques work here as well. And finally, common ground having common experiences, background values or other ailments makes you more persuadable. This type of manipulation is especially dangerous. If we are the type of person that cares about other people. And the more we do, the more easily we fall into this trap.

This is because to an extent, we crave elevation and understanding from others. Therefore, when others show that understanding, we are more likely to do things for them because we feel validated. So protection against this type of manipulation mostly comes from realizing that honestly, everything that the other side is saying can be a complete lie or a fabrication or just not drawing conclusions based on the similarity. So you have the similarity with me. OK, so what, for example, they say you seem to be similar to me or like me in this you play football like me. You went to Harvard University like me and so on.

And you ask, OK, where's the proof? Instead of just being impressed or someone says, I understand that you really want to find an honest salesman or whatever it is. And you say, OK, so what? So it's finding your tendency to assume that we do have commonalities. And realizing that the person may be faking it. What are some examples of identification? Manipulation? The first is social selling. You will surely have received messages of someone trying to sell you on Facebook or winkling. And they start by making friends. Then they start mentioning what they have in common.

The university, a company, an activity, etc. and then they try to beat you to something. So first they identify with you and then they try to pitch you customer support. Empathy is another type in every cLass interaction. The other side eventually is going to say, I understand this is hard or I understand this must be awkward or thank you for waiting. They are using empathy in an automated manner so that you feel understood and decrease your aggression. Ironically, when you realize that they're not using this in an honest way, when you hear this kind of empathy, you'll maybe become even more angry instead of issuing. Understood.

And finally, real estate agents, in order to persuade and sell a lot of real estate agents, will ask about your life events and then tell you about similar ones. So then they can say something like, oh, you're having your first year with me. Tell you about when I had mine or, oh, you're switching jobs. Let me tell you about when I switched jobs, because you now have something in common with them in the. And sell you more easily. What are our key takeaways here? The first is that identification manipulation consists of trying to fabricate ground or emphasize the one that already exists. This increases likeability with the other side. It's not always authentic. Commonalities can be authentic or not. But the key here is that most people never doubt them.

When someone tells you, oh, I also did this, you have a tendency to just believe them and assume that commonality exists. And this is how people get manipulated by people who easily fake commonalities. There are several types of elements in common that can be manipulated. Someone can claim to have similar experiences, values, traits, contacts, universities, jobs, among other things. So as we see, identification manipulation is fought by either not believing these commonalities or just realizing that just because someone has something in common with you, it doesn't mean that you should trust them more. You need the capacity to say, OK, so I have a kid and you have a kid as well. So what? Or you went to the same university as me. So what? This is how you fight it.

Identification Manipulation in Startups

Identification manipulation can be used with employees, investors or any other type of stakeholder. But it's especially present with clients. This is because the more effectively the startup solves the user's needs. The more successful it is. So besides just solving the need, showing that they understand, the customer's point of view helps sell and grow. So saying, for example, do you have this in this pain? We can help you achieve this and this that you want. And this can be then by emphasizing common beliefs, experiences, life events or others, regardless of whether the founding team actually has those in common or is just pretending to.

So, for example, a startup that is serving insurance clients may be made up of insurance industry founders as well, or they may just do very good research and really understand what insurance companies are looking for and usually for every startup that really understands their customers needs. And they're selling something widget. There is another one or even 10 that pretend to understand those needs, but are really just selling vaporware. So can this ID be justified or just manipulation? ID manipulation can also be leveraged in real time with investors or clients or partners who are mirroring or giving. So mirroring their words or their gestures to make them feel more at ease or using giving is either symbolic, such as opening the door for them, getting them a coffee or voluntarily sharing certain information in order to create a sense of obligation to give back to the other person.

Fact Manipulation

Fact manipulation is one of the most used types, arguably the most used type of manipulation consists of either lying about facts or changing them so that they appear to be something else. You can round numbers up, you can change compounding rates, or if everything else fails, you can just lie about the numbers. Let's take a look at these examples and more. This is one of the most basic types of manipulation, but it's still so important to cover. You can always manipulate the facts of something to make it look better or worse. This can involve changing numbers, weights, times, scores in other facts, which all can manipulate people into taking different actions. You can hide numbers.

You can change numbers. Or you can change the sample sizes to manipulate what they mean. There is some overlap between this in context manipulation, which is where you change what you compare something to in order to change how good it looks. For example, you have a twenty dollar book, right? If you compare it to ten dollar books. It is very expensive. But if you say it's a technical manual, most technical manuals are around 70 dollars, then suddenly it seems super cheap. And you didn't change anything about the product. Just the comparison. So there is some overlap here. In many cases, changing the perception of facts or omitting something also changes the comparison that the person makes. But in terms of fact manipulation itself, there are usually a couple of ways to do this.

The first is omitting facts by having certain numbers. You can change all the other numbers if your manager is trying to manipulate you into thinking you're the worst performer in the team. Instead of comparing you with all other performers, they can just compare you to the top three people. And if you're not one of them, obviously you're going to seem worse. The second is misleading statistics. You can manipulate sample sizes or data sections or even round numbers up to make things seem different. For example, let's say that you have a medication that works for two or three people. That's a sixty six point six success rate. But with three people, you can't really draw any conclusions. That doesn't stop people from using techniques like this.

The number is right technically, but it's not significant. And finally, the very basics: actually lying about the facts, forging or changing certain numbers, dates or other facts, that manipulation can occur in any area of life for any purpose. For example, a company can change their accounting numbers. They seem to be in better shape when a politician can change the job numbers to get more votes because the situation seems to be better or someone can change the results in a company to seem to be a better performer.

The best protection against this type of manipulation is always to demand transparency about the alternatives in order to be able to compare with them. It's similar to what you would do first hand their manipulation, because in many cases, standard manipulation relies on modifying the criteria, which are facts or numbers. For example, if the accounting numbers of a company seem too good to be true, you want to ask about the accounting numbers of other years for the same company or maybe other companies in the same industry or even other industries. You want to use different comparisons to frame this set of numbers.

This helps put the facts into perspective, and in many cases, it reveals the manipulation. What are some examples of fact manipulation? The first is small samples. Small sample bias is a very present type of fact manipulation. Because with a few examples, you can draw any conclusion you want. As we just mentioned, two out of three people, sixty six point six percent. But it's not relevant. The most extreme case is drawing conclusions from just one example, which can be your case if a lot of people do this. They say, oh, I had a bad experience with this. So I bet that everyone did as well. And in their example are specific numbers.

This is a very creative one. Specific numbers are more persuasive and they convince more so saying that something because the thousand dollars makes the other person think, OK, this price is arbitrary. They just came up with it. But since that something costs nine hundred and sixty seven dollars, point forty three makes the person think that you had a specific scientific reason for it. And finally, the effects of medications in terms of big pharma also work here when a medication says this reduces this type of pain for 95 percent of people. But you have to ask which type of people under which conditions, because that is very important.

In most cases, you find out that it's only people with a specific set of conditions. What are our key takeaways here? The first is changing the facts. You can manipulate the facts of something to change how it is perceived. These can be obfuscated or actually forged both times. A big component of fact manipulation is the lack of a proper comparison to other facts without having a reference point. Anyone can make a set of facts seem better or worse because there is no comparison. But with the comparison, it's going to be a lot harder to make bad numbers look good.

And finally, this can be used in any area for any purpose, which makes it a necessity to always place facts in context, something essential anywhere at any time. So as we see, fack manipulation can only be fought by demanding transparency on the numbers and being clear about the comparisons, the assumptions and everything else surrounding the numbers presented.

Fact Manipulation in Startups

Fact manipulation can be easily performed in a fast growing startup, and in a way, it's always there to a degree. So let me explain. In a startup that is growing and changing so fast, the projections can easily change as well. So the facts stated to one investor or client can easily change. You can tell a client that this feature will be then moved into the next day. You hire a coder or you have a breakthrough in coding. So maybe now it's one month or maybe urgent bugs pop up and now it'll take three months. So the issue is why when you gave them that prediction? Not really.

But it's just that reality changes so fast that projections do as well. So fact manipulation is always present to the GUI for the same reason. Naturally, internal factors may have less weight as well. Reality is more malleable. So one day the company is doing well with some employees. Our problem is the rate the next day. Something bad occurs. And that promise is reversed. Maybe a client is not paying on time or the investment that you thought you would get is falling through or similar. This constantly changing context makes it a lot easier for fact manipulation to occur, because facts are a lot more malleable than in other areas of life to begin with.

But besides these natural facts can actually be manipulated in a hard way. Sales can be forged. You can lie to clients about features that you don't have. The growth numbers can be doctored. You can lie to an employee about a future raise that you know that you'll never give them so that they stay in many other possible variations. And again, in all of these situations, because the facts change so fast, people can get away with a lot more more easily.

Context Manipulation

Let's talk about context manipulation. I'm not sure if this is one of the most frequently used ones, but it is the most dangerous type of manipulation. In short, we have a tendency to look at other things to determine the value of something. It's relative and not absolute. So if you change what you compare something to, you change its value. Let's say that you have a 20 dollar book. If you compare it to other Tendler books in a bookstore, it seems very expensive. But if you say it's a technical manual and technical manuals usually cost around 70 dollars, then suddenly it seems super cheap. So based on the comparison, it seems to have very different values and you change nothing about the product itself.

And this can be used for products, for candidates, for people, for everything. It's an absolute persuasion superweapon. Let's take a look at how it works. One of the most devastating or possibly the most devastating types of manipulation is context manipulation. In short, when you change what you compare something to, you change its value. We tend to look at the value of something as relative and not absolute. So if you can't compare something to different options or to change the options, you create different comparisons in a different context. And all of these change the value of that change. The most basic example is this counts if something is the.

And it doesn't get expensive. But if something is 5000 dollars, but it's on discount for 20 percent of the original value for one thousand, then suddenly it seems like a bargain. And it seems much more attractive. In reality, the price may be exactly the same, and the actual store may be faking the discount. But the effect that they create on you is very different with the exact same product. And with the exact same price. There are multiple techniques here that consist of context manipulation. The first is contrast manipulation, contrasting against different things. The most used example is if you have a 24-Hour book, you can say it's a normal book and compare it to Tendler books to make it look expensive.

But you can also say it's a technical manual and compare it to other 70 technical manuals to make it look very cheap. You can also change the options by changing the specific options that are compared. You change what each one of them means. If you only have two software plans, for example, ten dollars and forty dollars, the former one seems very expensive. But if you have four options at ten dollars, forty dollars, 70 in maybe one hundred, then the forty Golar option doesn't seem very expensive at all. Another method is emphasizing the differences between things the worst of eight versus the best the be.

For example, if you're a candidate, you can ask your hiring manager, would you rather hire this person? That is not organized. It doesn't have this and it doesn't have this. Or would you rather hire me? Who has this certifiction, these qualifications and this experience? In reality, it's probable that both A and B have good and bad things. But when you just mention the bad things of one of them versus the good things of the other one, it sounds much better. And finally, we have the peak in effect, which is different. It's about a chapter itself. So this effect, the fans, that if you aren't strong in a chapter and you have a highlight during that chapter, people will remember the rest.

It's also a type of context manipulation, because if you can say the right things during that highlight and at the end when the rest of the chapter doesn't really matter, no matter how bad it may be, this type of manipulation happens because we have a tendency to compare different options in order to calculate the value of something. In other words, the person who controls the different options controls what we perceive. This is very used in marketing. What the other products don't have is precisely what you emphasize in yours.

Even if everything else is 99 percent similar, you think the only difference and you ruthlessly emphasize that, you know, your product seems completely different. This type of manipulation is one of the most pervasive institutions, because to find it, you have to actively realize that the options that people are giving you may be forged or that the comparison may be unfair. We usually tend to accept whatever options are given, and we have to start actively questioning them. For example, you see a software with three plans, with three payment options. One is for ten dollars. The other is forty hours. And the other is ninety dollars. There's the free dollar option.

Seems reasonable. Now, what if I tell you that these free plans have been manipulated by the person to make the middle one seem the most attractive? What do you think of these options now? Exactly. To be honest, this is one of the types of manipulation that requires the most practice to. Right. Because we're simply not used to questioning the options and the comparisons that other people give us. What are some examples of context manipulation? The first is the middle option when you're presented with a set of options. We tend to choose the middle one. So these are manipulated to guide people to the middle option, as we just saw in the previous chapter.

If you have ten dollars, forty dollars out of 90 people are going to choose the forty dollars. You can even change the 40 to 50 if you want, because people are always guided to the middle option. So you can fabricate the options to make the middle one seem the most attractive. Another example is defining something as low end, medium end or high end. For example, something that is medium and can be considered the best low cost option. Or it can also be considered the most affordable premium option without changing anything in the actual product or person. It's all about perception. And finally, extremes in a negotiation. There's a technique called extreme anchoring.

And this is used by throwing out an extreme of something that you want. So, for example, if you want a 10 percent raise, you want to ask for a 20 percent line because the person may refuse this 20 percent and knock you down to 10 percent. But now they are going to think that those 10 percent seem a lot better because they seem a lot better by comparison. If you just say that it's 10, it sounds OK. But if you say it's 20 and they knock it down to 10, it sounds a lot more affordable. What are our key takeaways here? The first is that context is crucial. We tend to compare things to determine their value. So when the comparison is tampered with, so is the value that we attribute to something.

Whoever controls that comparison almost controls the value of something by association. The second is that you can almost cut, copy and paste the options, or literally, just like in a document editor options can be changed, can be added or removed entirely to control the specific option set that we use for the comparison. And with every change that we make, the perception that the person has is different. And finally, this can happen in any medium. This can be used not just to compare different types of information, but also for communication and chapter, such as the picture of the fact if the highlight and the end are strong. Everything else in that chapter is forgotten by comparison.

So you can use it to make one option seem valuable in the South, but also to make part of a chapter seem valuable compared to the rest of it. So as we see, context manipulation is one of the hardest types to fight, because you have to think what if the options presented are manipulated or what if the context that is being presented is not the real one at all. You have to not only remove the relative value and look at the absolute value, but you have to, in some cases, look at the relative value compared to other things, which honestly we just don't do in our everyday lives. This is possibly the hardest type of manipulation to fight.

Context Manipulation in Startups

Context manipulation is present in multiple areas of startups and naturally to different possibilities that these can include. First, the company is a market. The total and addressable markets of a startup can be tailored and selected to make up the most attractive numbers for investors. Peter Thiel talks about this in the book, The Zero to One. Big companies want to seem small to avoid regulation and taxes. So they changed their target market and industry to seem smaller. For example, Google was not advertising, we were just search advertising, which is a lot lower in small companies that want to see big. So they target bigger markets that they will actually never serve when their real market is only a segment of that.

Remember, change what you compare yourself to and you change your perception. Then the company's comparisons also come in here. Many startups market themselves as comparisons or analogies, which makes them easier to understand. For example, Uber for ABC. It also works as effort manipulation because people immediately get it. For example, if you tell people that you're a logistics company focused on the efficient delivery of medical supplies, they may get it or not. But if you say you're the Uber of medical supplies, they just get it. And they even assume all types of good things about your startup based on the comparison, such as the quality of the transportation, the quality of the application and so on.

This is especially useful for investors to grasp what the company bets in, finally. Naturally, the companies associations also come in here. Many startups associate themselves with big companies or universities just to seem more reputable, even if the relationship is quite weak. For example, saying we have to x Google founders or two Harvard MBA advisors. And so what? These have zero consequence in terms of the startups performance. But just due to the association, they make it seem a lot higher quality.

Labeling Manipulation

Let's take a look at the labeling manipulation. This is a very simple but very powerful type of manipulation. What you essentially do is when you attribute a name or a label to something in specific, you can change its value with that label. For example, we say that a co-worker did bad on the project. Somebody may label them as destructive and that the label will tend to stick no matter what they do. They are going to be considered a distracted person or an airhead or someone that doesn't care about the details, or someone can even label them as a failure. And now it doesn't matter what they do, they are going to be seen as a failure. This is just one example of labeling manipulation. Let's take a look at this example and more.

Another devastating type of manipulation includes changing the names and the labels that you give to labels in specific. Whether they're right or wrong, this is the reason why once the label has been placed, it's very hard to roll it back. It's not impossible, but it is very hard on top of that. Labels have a tendency to spread very easily, and this can seriously amplify their effect. For example, if there is a boy at work that labels someone as incompetent or clumsy in a work setting in other similar people, start calling that person Binit label as well. That effect is going to escalate very quickly and the label becomes very hard to remove specific types of manipulating labels. Including the most frequent one is Bohème labeling someone a failure, incompetent or others, especially when multiple people do it.

Then the presence or absence of names giving someone or something, your name humanizes it in removing that name, dehumanizes it, for example. Knowing someone's name is what makes them stop being a stranger and immediately start being someone that you can take seriously. Likewise, removing a person's name and just calling them the other Qualys or the supplier and so on removes all human traits from that person and it changes how you treat them. Then stereotypes which are nothing more than labels that oversimplify whole groups of people. And finally, scientific sounding words saying that you have a test or a hypothesis or make something sound more sophisticated than it actually is.

The manipulation of names and labels works very well due to perceived effort. Let me explain. We all have a tendency to simplify things in order to reduce the complexity of them in our minds. This is evolutionary. We want to conserve energy. So what happens is that simplistic names or labels present an opportunity to simplify something. We can identify a person or thing by using less information. So we take that opportunity. And in many cases, we accept the label without stopping to ask if that label is valid or not in the first place. We just think it's a handy mental shortcut and I'll take it. So if someone at work, for example, has several skills, but lately has not been creative at all and just focuses on repetitive work in someone who labels them a robot, for example.

And although that label is borderline offensive, by the way, if you adopt it in your mind, you have just reduced the person to that label and you have eliminated all other characteristics that they have. This person in your mind is just a robot. Now, nothing else. Finding this bias can only occur when you actively question the names and the labels associated with something. You want to have the courage to realize that that name or label may be oversimplifying something and that there may be more to the person or thing than the label. So, for example, does this name or label represent the whole person or the whole thing? Does this name or label eliminate important aspects that are not included in it? There's this name or label even accurately represented, among other questions.

What are some examples of labeling manipulation? The first is titles. Someone being a doctor, a master or having another title makes them seem important and intelligent, even if they're not. Don't get me wrong, I'm not bashing doctors. I'm just saying that in many cases, people attribute authority to that person due to the title and not due to their actual skills. The label is manipulated to make the person seem more important. Another example is fake news. It works in a similar manner. Fake news oversimplifies things because it doesn't need to hold up under scrutiny like real news. That's the way for definition, because it's simpler, catches on much quicker and travels faster because it doesn't need to be revised.

This is actually a concept called simplistic scalability. The more simplistic that something is, even if it is in the wrong way, the faster it spreads. And finally, an example from law, the defendant's name in a court saying you will notice that in court, the prosecution lawyer never mentions the defendant's name. They don't say, oh, Mr. Marks did this. They say the defendant did this because they're trying to dehumanize them. And the defense lawyer does the opposite, always using their name as much as possible, saying, Mr. Marks, we're not want to do this or Mr. Mock thinks this. And so on. Each side is trying to make the defendant more human and less human, respectively. Each side is trying to leverage the precise opposite effect of this manipulation.

What are our key takeaways here? The first is that we want to simplify by nature names and Weebles work because we want to reduce complexity and boil things down to simple names and definitions. So we accept them, even if they are completely wrong, as long as they simplify. We tend to adopt them. Names and labels are one of the most devastating types of manipulation because they're sticky. It's very hard to take them back after the deed. Once you label that person in your office, the robot, even if they do countless creative things and even if they actively fight the label, that label is going to stick for a long time. It's not impossible to take back, but it is extremely hard. And finally, this can only be fought by questioning the process every time that we hear a simplistic waybill or a name.

And it sounds so easy that we want to adopt it. We have to stop ourselves to check whether this simplified label is actually useful or not. We have to question if that model is accurate. We have to fight that temptation in a way. So as we've seen, labeling manipulation is very powerful. Not just the type of names that you attribute to something, change its value, but even the absence or the presence of those names. It's a very dangerous type of manipulation because those labels tend to stick and they tend to spread.

Labeling Manipulation in Startups

Labeling manipulation can be used in startups for different purposes. First, competing solutions can be labeled in a negative manner to make them look worse. You can say our competition is full of bugs. It's clunky. It's slow. They don't have dedicated founders. They don't understand the customer and so on. This can also be a type of context manipulation. Since you're comparing yourself with them. But technically, it's also labeling manipulation because that label will stick.

If you make a 30 minute chapter where you just state that the competition is incompetent, slow and so on. At the end of the day, your clients will just think that subconsciously and even if their current solution is perfect, the moment they make a mistake, they are going to think, oh, they are incompetent. After all, remember, labels are extremely sticky. Then employees or clients can also be labeled in a negative manner to gain support for firing or replacing them. Saying something like, John is a failure, is not sociable and they are mediocre.

You can even just use one of these if you want to get an employee fired. Just call them a failure in public. And every time that you make a small mistake, you repeat that. And soon, everybody is going to start thinking, failure, failure, failure. Unfortunately, this is a type of bullying that shouldn't be done, but does occur. And finally, the product itself can be labeled with specific words to create that impression, even if it doesn't open at all. So you can say our product is the fastest or our startup has the smartest people and so on. You can combine this with effort, manipulation, taking a word like simple or fast, and then just labeling yourself repeatedly using that word, even when your product is not speedy at all. The label is going to stick and people will give you the benefit of the doubt.

Conclusion

We are now at the end of how manipulation works, Of course. Wow. We've covered several different times. Which of the following let's take a minute just to recap all of these different types of manipulation and how to fight them. We have now arrived at the conclusion of the Book. Our biggest goal for this Book was to illustrate the different ways in which manipulation is used, including but not limited to how cognitive biases are exploited, including false contrasts, mental effort, availability, biases and others. How people manipulate through pressure by intimidating, using emotional blackmail, creating false and others.

How the facts themselves can be discarded or obfuscated by having different standards, contrasting things to change their apparent value or just lying, or how identification can manipulate, making someone feel understood or using fake commonalities so that they like you more. By now, you should be much more adept at identifying and stopping manipulation when it's used against you. You should know which mechanisms are in place and how to prevent them. So a short recap for our disBook. We've explored nine key ways in which manipulation is used. The first was consistency, manipulation.

Getting someone to state something or to do something which triggers a consistency trap in their mind and makes them act in alignment with what they said or did. Then emotional manipulation, throwing tantrums or having emotional reactions in relying on their side, feeling guilty and taking the blame for your reaction or just triggering an emotion in them after that effort, manipulation, reducing the perceived effort of something by using little effort, words, reducing the options or preempting uncertainty.

Then came standard manipulation. Having different standards or criteria for different things, which changes their value or just making exceptions for certain people. After that, pressure, manipulation, using some kind of pressure on the other person, be it intimidating them, creating false urgency or through other mechanisms or crashing them into action. Then can ID manipulation make the other side feel like you understand them or that you share these traits, experiences or values in order to make them more enforceable after that? In fact, manipulation, obfuscating or lying about actual facts in order to make a situation seem different.

By changing the chapter of the facts, you change the value of things. Then context manipulation, arguably the most powerful time, changing what you can bear something to. Or changing the options in order to change its relative value. Highlighting different parts. Changing the options and more in the last time. Labeling manipulation, changing the label, attribute it to something or even removing it entirely changes the interpretation that people have of that something for a long time. And it can spread easily with a summary.

We can now see how manipulation works, Of course. I hope that disBook has helped you in identifying and stopping different types of manipulation in your life. Thank you so much for reading. So we close how manipulation works Of course. I hope that this Book has given you some ideas on how to not be manipulated, as well as how to fight these effects in everyday life. And maybe you can help both yourself and others in finding manipulation. I hope that I have given you some useful tools and knowledge about this topic. Thank you so much for reading.

Bonus

Congratulations on finishing the Book. You know, you may ask what's next? I have three quick tips for you. Ask questions. Take any doubts that you may still have. Go to the chapter and ask that question because I and other students can help with some knowledge.

Number three, make sure to check out additional links. I have a YouTube channel with samples from other Books, but also some videos on persuasion, negotiation, communication, and some other technical topics which may be of interest. You also have my booking page in case you're interested in coaching or consulting. And last but not least, if you're reading this Book as part of a masterclass, then just like a connecting flight at the airport, this is not your final destination and has to the next gate. Thank you so much for reading.